QUANTUM OPERATING SYSTEMS FOR ADVANCED EMBEDDED SYSTEMS: A GUIDE FOR EMBEDDED ENGINEERS

SASIKUMAR C

Made with ♥ on the Notion Press Platform
www.notionpress.com

To the pioneers of quantum computing and embedded systems,
whose relentless pursuit of innovation has brought us to the dawn of a new computing era.

To the engineers, researchers, and developers,
who dream beyond the limits of classical computation and dare to build the impossible.

To the educators and students,
who continuously seek knowledge and push the boundaries of technology.

And to my parents,my beloved wife Surya and my super champ Ritvik , friends, and mentors,
whose unwavering support and encouragement have made this journey possible.

This book is for all those who believe that the future of computing is not just faster but fundamentally different.

Contents

Foreword

The world of embedded systems is evolving at an unprecedented pace. From microcontrollers to AI-driven automation, embedded computing has continually adapted to the growing demands of industries such as automotive, healthcare, aerospace, and telecommunications. However, we are now reaching the limits of classical computing, where conventional architectures struggle to process complex real-time computations efficiently.

This is where quantum computing steps in—not as a replacement for classical systems, but as an augmentation that opens new possibilities. The integration of quantum computing with embedded systems is not a distant dream; it is an emerging reality that will redefine how we approach optimization, cryptography, machine learning, and data processing at the edge.

This book, Quantum Operating Systems in Advanced Embedded Systems, is a crucial step toward bridging the gap between quantum computing and embedded engineering. It demystifies quantum concepts, explores hybrid quantum-classical architectures, and provides practical insights into how Quantum OS can be designed, implemented, and optimized for real-world applications.

The author has done an exceptional job of breaking down complex topics into digestible, engaging content. With clear explanations, real-world examples, and a forward-thinking approach, this book will serve as a valuable resource for engineers, researchers, and professionals eager to explore the next generation of embedded computing.

As we stand at the frontier of a quantum revolution, this book will guide you through the principles, challenges, and opportunities that lie ahead. Whether you are an embedded systems engineer, a software developer, or a technology enthusiast, you will find this book both enlightening and inspiring.

Welcome to the future of embedded quantum computing.

PREFACE

The field of embedded systems has long been driven by the pursuit of efficiency, reliability, and scalability. From industrial automation to consumer electronics, embedded computing has played a critical role in shaping modern technology. However, as computational demands increase—particularly in artificial intelligence, cybersecurity, and real-time decision-making—classical computing architectures are beginning to reach their limits.

Quantum computing, with its unique ability to process complex problems exponentially faster than classical systems, offers a revolutionary path forward. While much of the focus on quantum computing has been on large-scale applications in finance, cryptography, and scientific research, its potential in embedded systems remains largely unexplored. This book aims to bridge that gap by introducing Quantum Operating Systems (Quantum OS) and their role in hybrid quantum-classical embedded computing.

The motivation for writing this book comes from the growing need to integrate quantum capabilities into real-world applications where traditional processors struggle. Whether in autonomous vehicles, edge computing, IoT security, or high-performance simulations, Quantum OS will play a crucial role in shaping the future of embedded computing.

This book is structured to guide readers from foundational quantum principles to practical implementations of Quantum OS. Each chapter builds upon key concepts, providing clear explanations, real-world use cases, and technical insights. The goal is to empower embedded engineers, software developers, and technology enthusiasts to navigate this emerging field with confidence.This book exapain provides a high-level overview of the core principles of quantum computing and its potential applications in embedded systems.

As quantum computing continues to advance, the intersection of quantum and embedded systems will open doors to new technological frontiers. I hope this book serves as a valuable resource in understanding, experimenting with, and contributing to this exciting evolution.

[Sasikumar C]

[26-02-2025]

Acknowledgements

The journey of writing this book has been both challenging and rewarding, and it would not have been possible without the support, guidance, and inspiration of many individuals and organizations.

First and foremost, I would like to express my deepest gratitude to the pioneers of quantum computing and embedded systems, whose groundbreaking research and innovations have laid the foundation for this emerging field. Their work continues to inspire engineers, researchers, and developers to push the boundaries of what is possible.

I extend my sincere appreciation to my mentors, colleagues, and collaborators who have provided invaluable insights, constructive feedback, and technical discussions throughout the development of this book. Your expertise and encouragement have greatly enriched its content.

To my family and friends, your unwavering support, patience, and encouragement have been instrumental in this journey. Your belief in my work has been my greatest motivation.

I would also like to thank the publishers, editors, and reviewers who have helped shape this book into its final form. Your keen eye for detail and dedication to excellence have ensured that the content is both accessible and impactful.

Finally, to the readers—engineers, students, and technology enthusiasts—who are passionate about the future of computing, thank you for embarking on this journey with me. I hope this book serves as a valuable resource in your exploration of Quantum OS in embedded systems and inspires you to contribute to this rapidly evolving field.

With heartfelt appreciation,

Sasikumar C

26-02-2025

PROLOGUE

The world is on the brink of a new computing revolution. For decades, embedded systems have powered everything from household appliances to space exploration. These systems, designed for efficiency and precision, have pushed the limits of classical computing. But as we step into an era driven by artificial intelligence, real-time decision-making, and complex problem-solving, traditional embedded architectures are struggling to keep up.

Imagine an autonomous vehicle navigating a chaotic cityscape. It must process vast amounts of sensor data, predict pedestrian movements, and make split-second decisions—all while ensuring safety and efficiency. Or consider a cybersecurity system tasked with detecting and neutralizing advanced cyber threats in real-time. What if there was a way to process these tasks exponentially faster?

Enter Quantum Operating Systems (Quantum OS)—a groundbreaking fusion of quantum computing and embedded technology. Unlike classical systems, quantum computers leverage the principles of superposition, entanglement, and quantum parallelism to tackle problems that were once considered unsolvable. Quantum OS acts as the bridge, enabling seamless interaction between quantum processors and classical embedded systems.

This book is not about replacing classical embedded computing with quantum technology. Instead, it explores how hybrid quantum-classical systems will redefine computing at the edge, optimizing tasks such as route optimization, cryptographic security, medical diagnostics, and AI-driven decision-making.

The journey ahead is complex, but the potential is limitless. Embedded engineers, developers, and researchers now stand at the forefront of an exciting new frontier. This book will guide you through the foundations, architectures, and real-world applications of Quantum OS, empowering you to be part of the next computing revolution.

The question is no longer if quantum computing will impact embedded systems—but how soon you will be ready for it.

Welcome to the future

I

Chapter 1: Fundamentals of Quantum Computing for Embedded Engineers

Imagine a world where the devices around you—your smartwatch, your car, even your refrigerator—are not just smart, but quantum smart. These devices would process information at speeds that defy classical physics, solve complex problems in the blink of an eye, and operate with an efficiency that seems almost magical. This is not science fiction; this is the promise of quantum computing in embedded systems.

But before we can build this quantum-powered future, we need to understand the building blocks of quantum computing. For embedded engineers, this means stepping into a realm where bits are no longer just 0s and 1s, where particles can exist in multiple states simultaneously, and where the very act of observing a system can change its behavior. It's a world that challenges our classical intuition, but one that holds immense potential for transforming the way we design and interact with embedded systems.

In this chapter, we'll embark on a journey to demystify quantum computing for embedded engineers. We'll start with the basics: what are qubits, and how do they differ from classical bits? We'll explore the strange and fascinating principles of superposition and entanglement, and we'll see how quantum gates and circuits can perform computations that are impossible for classical systems. Along the way, we'll address the practical challenges of working with quantum systems, from maintaining qubit coherence to dealing with the inevitable noise and errors that arise in quantum computations.

By the end of this chapter, you'll have a solid foundation in the fundamentals of quantum computing, and you'll be ready to explore how these principles can be applied to the design of advanced embedded systems. So, let's take the first step into the quantum realm and discover how the strange and powerful world of quantum computing can revolutionize the field of embedded systems.

Quantum Bits (Qubits)

Qubits are the building blocks of quantum computing. Unlike classical bits, which can be either 0 or 1, qubits can exist in a superposition of both states simultaneously.

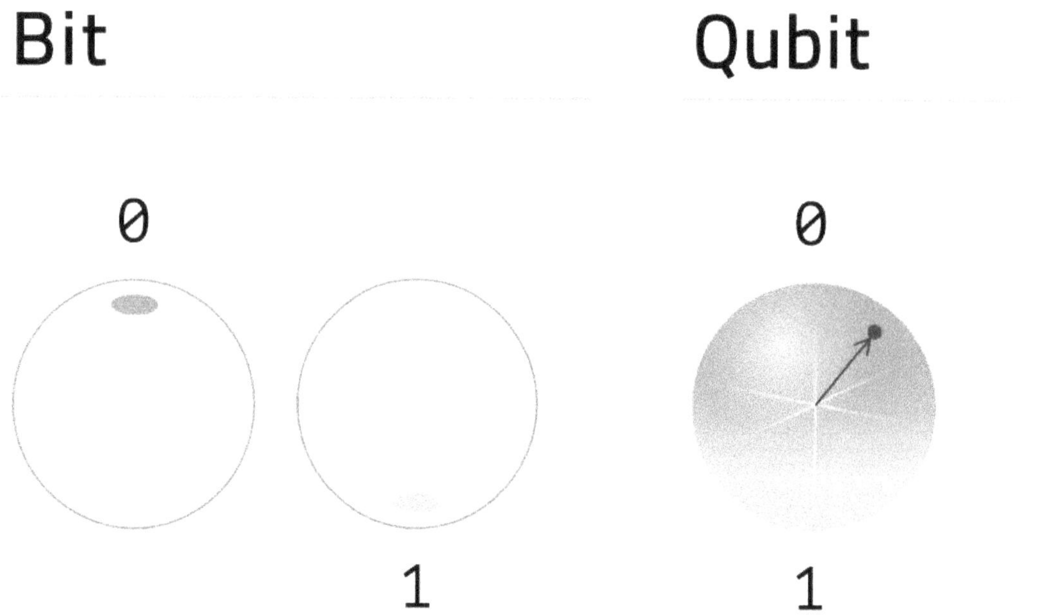

Visualizing a bit and a qubit.

Example: Imagine a qubit as a spinning coin. While it's spinning, it's neither heads nor tails but a combination of both. Only when it lands (is measured) does it "decide" its state.

Data Point: IBM's 127-qubit Eagle processor demonstrates how qubits can be scaled up for complex computations.

Clarification: Superposition allows a quantum computer to process multiple possibilities at once, making it exponentially faster for certain tasks like optimization and searching.

Quantum Gates and Circuits

Quantum gates manipulate qubits through operations like the Hadamard gate (creates superposition) and the CNOT gate (entangles qubits).

Example: A simple quantum circuit might use a Hadamard gate to create a superposition, followed by a CNOT gate to entangle two qubits. This is the basis for quantum algorithms like Grover's search.

Anecdote: In 2019, Google's Sycamore processor used quantum gates to achieve "quantum supremacy" by solving a problem in 200 seconds that would take a supercomputer 10,000 years.

Clarification: Quantum circuits are sequences of quantum gates that perform specific computations. Unlike classical circuits, quantum circuits are probabilistic, meaning they provide a range of possible outcomes.

Quantum Entanglement and Superposition

Entanglement allows qubits to be correlated in such a way that the state of one qubit instantly influences the state of another, no matter the distance.

Example: In a quantum sensor, entangled qubits can measure magnetic fields with unprecedented precision, useful for medical imaging or mineral exploration.

Data Point: China's Micius satellite demonstrated quantum entanglement over 1,200 kilometers, a milestone for quantum communication.

Clarification: Entanglement is a key resource for quantum computing, enabling tasks like quantum teleportation and secure communication.

Quantum vs. Classical Computing

Quantum computers excel at problems involving large datasets, optimization, and simulations, while classical computers are better for linear tasks.

Example: A quantum computer could optimize traffic flow in a smart city by evaluating all possible routes simultaneously, whereas a classical computer would evaluate them one by one.

Anecdote: D-Wave's quantum annealers have been used by Volkswagen to optimize traffic flow in Beijing, reducing travel times by 20%.

Clarification: Quantum computers are not universally faster than classical computers; they excel at specific tasks like factoring large numbers (Shor's algorithm) and searching unsorted databases (Grover's algorithm).

II

Chapter 2: Embedded Systems in the Quantum Era

Embedded systems are the unsung heroes of the modern world. They power everything from your smartphone to the avionics in an airplane, performing critical tasks with precision and reliability. But as the demands on these systems grow—faster processing, greater efficiency, enhanced security—classical computing is reaching its limits. Enter quantum computing, a technology that promises to push these limits far beyond what we thought possible.

In this chapter, we'll explore what it means to bring embedded systems into the quantum era. We'll start by examining the current challenges facing embedded systems: the relentless demand for more processing power, the need for energy efficiency in battery-powered devices, and the ever-present threat of cyberattacks. We'll then look at how quantum computing can address these challenges, offering new capabilities that were previously unimaginable.

But integrating quantum computing into embedded systems is no small feat. It requires a deep understanding of both quantum and classical technologies, as well as innovative approaches to system design. We'll discuss the potential of quantum-enhanced hardware, from quantum processors to quantum sensors, and we'll explore how these technologies can be integrated into existing embedded systems.

By the end of this chapter, you'll have a clear understanding of the opportunities and challenges that quantum computing presents for embedded systems. You'll see how the quantum era is not just a distant dream, but a tangible future that is already beginning to take shape. So, let's dive in and explore how quantum computing can transform the world of embedded systems.

Google Quantum AI Compute Device

Current Challenges in Embedded Systems

Embedded systems face limitations in processing power, energy efficiency, and scalability.

Example: A drone's flight controller must process sensor data in real-time while conserving battery life—a challenge for classical systems.

Data Point: The global IoT market is expected to reach $1.6 trillion by 2025, increasing demand for efficient embedded systems.

Clarification: Quantum computing can address these challenges by performing complex computations more efficiently, reducing the need for powerful (and power-hungry) classical processors.

Quantum-Enhanced Hardware

Quantum sensors, such as atomic clocks and magnetometers, offer higher precision and lower power consumption.

Example: Quantum magnetometers are used in autonomous vehicles to detect subtle changes in the Earth's magnetic field for navigation.

Anecdote: NASA's Cold Atom Lab uses quantum sensors in space to study microgravity effects on atoms.

Clarification: Quantum sensors leverage phenomena like superposition and entanglement to achieve unprecedented levels of precision, making them ideal for applications like medical imaging and environmental monitoring.

Quantum-Enabled Use Cases

Quantum computing can enhance real-time processing, optimization, and machine learning in embedded systems.

Example: Quantum machine learning algorithms can improve image recognition in medical devices, enabling faster diagnosis.

Data Point: Quantum machine learning is projected to grow at a CAGR of 30% from 2023 to 2030.

Clarification: Quantum machine learning algorithms can process large datasets more efficiently, enabling real-time decision-making in applications like autonomous vehicles and industrial automation.

Challenges in Integration

Integrating quantum technologies into embedded systems requires overcoming hardware limitations and high costs.

Example: A startup developing quantum-enhanced IoT devices faced challenges in miniaturizing quantum processors.

Anecdote: Rigetti Computing is working on hybrid quantum-classical systems to make quantum integration more practical.

Clarification: One of the main challenges is the need for cryogenic cooling systems to maintain qubit coherence, which can be difficult to implement in small, portable devices.

III

Chapter 3: Quantum Operating Systems in Embedded Systems

Embedded computing has evolved from simple microcontrollers to complex, AI-driven processors. However, as AI, cybersecurity, and optimization problems demand more computational power, classical computing is hitting its limits. Quantum computing offers an unprecedented solution, but integrating it into embedded systems requires a new kind of operating system: Quantum OS. This chapter introduces the core concepts of Quantum OS, the challenges it aims to solve, and how embedded engineers can start exploring this transformative technology.

Classical vs. Quantum Processing

Classical bits operate in binary states (0 or 1), while qubits exist in superposition, representing multiple states simultaneously.

Example: A classical bit is like a light switch—it's either on or off. A qubit, however, is like a dimmer switch, capable of being in multiple states at once.

Clarification: Superposition enables quantum parallelism, allowing quantum computers to process multiple possibilities simultaneously. This is the foundation of quantum speedup.

Quantum-Classical Hybrid Computing

Quantum computing accelerates specific tasks, while classical processors handle general computing.

Example: In a self-driving car, a quantum processor could optimize the route, while a classical processor controls the steering.

Data Point: D-Wave's quantum annealing has been shown to optimize logistics routes 100x faster than classical methods.

Use Cases for Quantum OS

Quantum OS provides advantages in cryptography, AI optimization, and real-time data processing.

Example: A quantum-enhanced firewall could detect anomalies in network traffic faster than classical intrusion detection systems.

Anecdote: In 2019, Google's Sycamore processor performed a calculation in 200 seconds that would take a supercomputer 10,000 years.

Challenges in Implementation

Developing Quantum OS involves overcoming hardware instability, quantum error correction, and software adaptability.

Example: A startup developing quantum-enhanced IoT devices faced challenges in miniaturizing quantum processors.

Clarification: Quantum error correction is essential for maintaining qubit coherence, but it requires additional qubits and complex algorithms.

The Road Ahead

Emerging trends in Quantum OS include advancements in quantum hardware, software frameworks, and hybrid architectures.

Example: Microsoft's Azure Quantum and IBM's Qiskit runtime are leading the way in Quantum OS development.

Clarification: Engineers need to develop skills in quantum programming languages like Qiskit, Cirq, and PennyLane to contribute to Quantum OS development.

IV

Chapter 4: The Breaking Point – Why Quantum OS is Essential

As embedded systems continue to evolve, engineers are encountering limitations in processing power, efficiency, and security. Quantum computing presents a potential solution, but why is it essential right now? This chapter explores the breaking point—where classical systems fail—and illustrates how quantum computing is stepping in to redefine embedded computing.

Moore's Law and the End of Classical Scaling

Transistor miniaturization is slowing down, and new computing paradigms are necessary.

Example: The latest Intel processors are struggling to achieve significant performance gains due to physical limitations.

Clarification: Quantum computing offers a way to bypass these limitations by leveraging quantum mechanics.

The Need for Quantum Speedup

Quantum computing provides significant acceleration in processing complex computations.

Example: Quantum annealing can solve optimization problems like the traveling salesman problem exponentially faster than classical methods.

Data Point: D-Wave's quantum annealers have been used by over 250 organizations for optimization tasks.

Industrial Use Cases

Quantum computing is essential in sectors like finance, aerospace, logistics, and healthcare.

Example: In healthcare, quantum computing can optimize drug discovery by simulating molecular interactions.

Anecdote: Volkswagen used quantum annealing to optimize bus routes in Lisbon, reducing fuel consumption by 15%.

Quantum Advantage

Quantum computing enables unique problem-solving approaches, such as quantum annealing for optimization tasks.

Example: A quantum-enhanced drone uses Grover's algorithm to optimize its flight path in real-time.

Clarification: Quantum advantage refers to the point where quantum computers outperform classical computers for specific tasks.

When to Use Quantum Computing

Quantum computing is most beneficial for problems involving large datasets, optimization, and simulations.

Example: Quantum machine learning algorithms can improve image recognition in medical devices, enabling faster diagnosis.

Clarification: Classical computing remains superior for linear tasks and general-purpose computing.

V

Chapter 5: Fundamentals of Quantum Computing for Embedded Engineers

Quantum computing introduces a radically different way of processing information compared to classical computers. For embedded engineers, understanding quantum principles is the first step in leveraging Quantum OS. This chapter simplifies quantum computing fundamentals, explaining key concepts like qubits, superposition, entanglement, and quantum circuits.If you've programmed microcontrollers, you know every bit counts. Now, imagine bits that exist in multiple states simultaneously—this is the power of quantum computing. In this chapter, we break down the core principles of quantum mechanics for embedded engineers and explore how they apply to Quantum OS development. From qubits and quantum parallelism to error correction and hybrid computing, this chapter provides the foundational knowledge you need to understand and leverage quantum computing in embedded systems.

Qubits vs. Classical Bits

Classical Bits: Represent binary states (0 or 1) and are the foundation of classical computing.

Example: A microcontroller processes data using classical bits, performing operations like addition, subtraction, and logic gates.

Qubits: Quantum bits that can exist in a superposition of 0 and 1, enabling quantum parallelism.

Example: A qubit can represent both 0 and 1 simultaneously, allowing a quantum computer to process multiple possibilities at once.

Clarification: Superposition is the foundation of quantum computing's speedup, enabling exponential processing power for certain tasks.

Data Point: IBM's 127-qubit Eagle processor demonstrates how qubits can be scaled up for complex computations.

Quantum Gates and Circuits

Quantum Gates: Operations that manipulate qubits, such as the Hadamard gate (creates superposition) and the CNOT gate (entangles qubits).

Example: A simple quantum circuit might use a Hadamard gate to create a superposition, followed by a CNOT gate to entangle two qubits.

Clarification: Quantum gates are the building blocks of quantum circuits, which perform specific computations.

Quantum Circuits: Sequences of quantum gates that perform computations. Unlike classical circuits, quantum circuits are probabilistic, meaning they provide a range of possible outcomes.

Example: Grover's algorithm uses quantum gates to search unsorted databases exponentially faster than classical algorithms.

Anecdote: In 2019, Google's Sycamore processor used quantum gates to achieve "quantum supremacy" by solving a problem in 200 seconds that would take a supercomputer 10,000 years.

Quantum Entanglement and Superposition

Superposition: Qubits can exist in multiple states simultaneously, enabling quantum parallelism.

Example: A quantum computer with 50 qubits can represent 2^50 (over a quadrillion) states simultaneously.

Clarification: Superposition allows quantum computers to explore multiple solutions at once, making them exponentially faster for certain tasks.

Entanglement: Qubits can be correlated in such a way that the state of one qubit instantly influences the state of another, no matter the distance.

Example: In a quantum sensor, entangled qubits can measure magnetic fields with unprecedented precision.

Data Point: China's Micius satellite demonstrated quantum entanglement over 1,200 kilometers, a milestone for quantum communication.

Clarification: Entanglement is a key resource for quantum computing, enabling tasks like quantum teleportation and secure communication.

Quantum vs. Classical Computing

Quantum Computing: Excels at problems involving large datasets, optimization, and simulations.

Example: A quantum computer could optimize traffic flow in a smart city by evaluating all possible routes simultaneously.

Anecdote: D-Wave's quantum annealers have been used by Volkswagen to optimize traffic flow in Beijing, reducing travel times by 20%.

Classical Computing: Better suited for linear tasks and general-purpose computing.

Example: Classical computers are still more efficient for tasks like word processing and web browsing.

Clarification: Quantum computers are not universally faster than classical computers; they excel at specific tasks like factoring large numbers (Shor's algorithm) and searching unsorted databases (Grover's algorithm).

Quantum Error Correction

Quantum Noise and Decoherence: Qubits are prone to errors due to environmental interference, making error correction essential.

Example: IBM's quantum processors use error correction codes to mitigate the effects of noise and decoherence.

Clarification: Quantum error correction requires additional qubits and complex algorithms, making it a significant challenge for embedded systems.

Error Correction Techniques: Methods like the surface code and stabilizer codes are used to maintain qubit coherence.

Example: A quantum-enhanced drone uses error correction to ensure accurate navigation in noisy environments.

Data Point: Error correction can improve qubit coherence by up to 50%, enabling longer computation times.

Hybrid Quantum-Classical Computing

Quantum and Classical Processors: Quantum processors handle complex tasks, while classical processors manage routine operations.

Example: In an autonomous vehicle, the quantum processor optimizes the route, while the classical processor controls the steering.

Clarification: Hybrid architectures enable efficient task offloading, balancing the strengths and limitations of quantum and classical computing.

Communication Protocols: Efficient communication between quantum and classical components is critical for hybrid systems.

Example: A quantum-enhanced IoT network uses classical protocols for data transmission and quantum protocols for encryption.

Data Point: The Quantum Internet Alliance is developing protocols for hybrid quantum-classical networks.

Building Blocks of a Quantum OS

Quantum Task Scheduling: Quantum tasks are prioritized and distributed in a hybrid computing environment.

Example: A quantum-enhanced drone uses a hybrid scheduler to balance real-time flight control with quantum optimization tasks.

Clarification: Quantum task scheduling requires balancing the strengths and limitations of quantum and classical processors.

Quantum Memory Management: Quantum registers differ from classical RAM, with unique constraints and capabilities.

Example: Quantum memory is volatile, requiring careful management to maintain qubit coherence.

Clarification: Memory management in Quantum OS involves handling both classical and quantum data formats.

VI

Chapter 6: Architectural Design of Quantum OS for Embedded Systems

A well-designed operating system is crucial to any computing platform, but Quantum OS presents new architectural challenges. How does it manage tasks, memory, and security? This chapter explores the unique architectural components of Quantum OS and how they redefine embedded system operations.From task scheduling to memory management, we'll delve into the design principles that make Quantum OS a transformative technology for embedded systems.

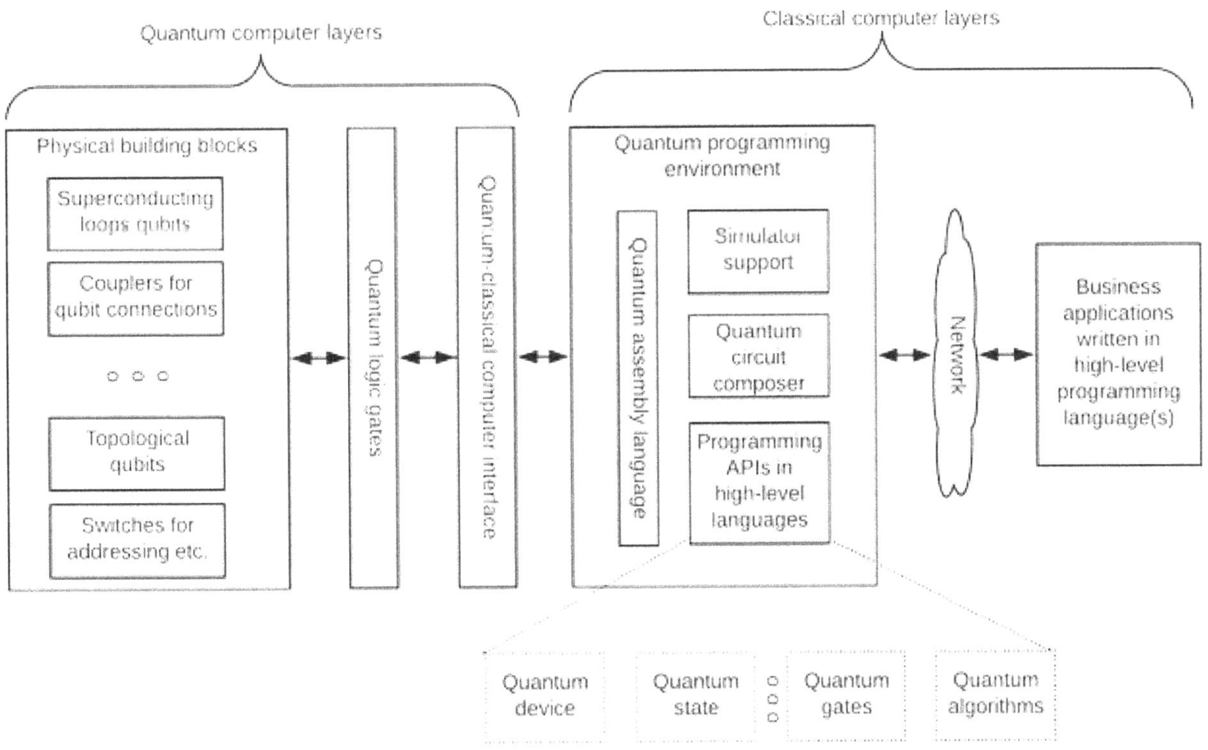

Architecture of quantum computing platform.

Task Scheduling in Quantum OS

Classical vs. Quantum Task Scheduling: Classical operating systems use deterministic scheduling, while Quantum OS must handle probabilistic quantum tasks.

Example: In an autonomous vehicle, the Quantum OS schedules quantum optimization tasks alongside classical real-time control tasks.

Clarification: Quantum tasks are non-deterministic, requiring hybrid schedulers that balance quantum and classical workloads.

Hybrid Scheduling: Quantum OS prioritizes quantum tasks within classical real-time constraints.

Example: A quantum-enhanced drone uses a hybrid scheduler to optimize its flight path while maintaining real-time responsiveness.

Data Point: Hybrid schedulers can improve task efficiency by up to 30% in quantum-classical systems.

Quantum Kernel:

Qubit Scheduling: Manages qubit allocation and scheduling for quantum computations, optimizing for minimal interference and coherence time.

Quantum Gate Management: Provides abstractions for quantum gates, handling their sequencing and error mitigation strategies.

Quantum State Representation: Implements efficient data structures to represent quantum states, considering the specific quantum hardware architecture.

Memory Management

Quantum Registers vs. Classical RAM: Quantum registers store qubits, which are volatile and prone to decoherence, unlike classical RAM.

Example: A Quantum OS must manage qubit coherence time, ensuring computations are completed before qubits lose their state.

Clarification: Quantum memory management involves handling both classical and quantum data formats, requiring specialized algorithms.

Quantum Error Correction: Quantum OS incorporates error correction techniques to maintain qubit stability.

Example: IBM's Quantum OS uses surface codes to correct errors in qubit states.

Data Point: Error correction can extend qubit coherence time by up to 50%, enabling longer computations.

Security in Quantum OS

Quantum Cryptography: Quantum OS leverages quantum principles like entanglement to create unbreakable encryption.

Example: A Quantum OS uses Quantum Key Distribution (QKD) to secure communication between IoT devices.

Clarification: QKD ensures that any attempt to intercept the encryption key alters the quantum state, alerting the system to the intrusion.

Post-Quantum Cryptography: Quantum OS integrates post-quantum cryptographic algorithms to resist quantum attacks.

Example: NIST-standardized algorithms like CRYSTALS-Kyber are used in Quantum OS to secure embedded systems.

Data Point: Post-quantum cryptography is projected to grow at a CAGR of 30% from 2023 to 2030.

Quantum Process Handling

Concurrent Execution Models: Quantum OS enables concurrent execution of quantum and classical tasks.

Example: A quantum-enhanced IoT device processes sensor data using quantum algorithms while running classical control tasks.

Clarification: Quantum OS must ensure low-latency communication between quantum and classical processors.

Quantum-Classical Communication: Efficient protocols are needed to transfer data between quantum and classical components.

Example: A Quantum OS uses optimized communication protocols to minimize latency in hybrid systems.

Data Point: The Quantum Internet Alliance is developing protocols for hybrid quantum-classical networks.

Existing Quantum OS Implementations

Microsoft's Azure Quantum: A cloud-based Quantum OS that provides tools for developing and deploying quantum applications.

Example: Azure Quantum is used to optimize supply chain logistics using quantum algorithms.

Clarification: Cloud-based Quantum OS platforms enable edge devices to access quantum resources remotely.

IBM's Qiskit Runtime: A Quantum OS framework for hybrid quantum-classical systems.

Example: Qiskit Runtime is used to prototype quantum-enhanced drones and autonomous vehicles.

Data Point: IBM's Q System One is a hybrid quantum-classical system designed for practical applications.

Key Architectural Components

Quantum Processing Unit (QPU) Interface:

Quantum Instruction Set: Define a set of quantum instructions that the OS can execute on the QPU. This includes gates, measurements, and error correction operations.

QPU Abstraction Layer: Create an abstraction layer that allows the OS to interact with different QPU architectures (e.g., superconducting qubits, trapped ions).

Classical-Quantum Hybrid Scheduler:

Task Scheduling: Develop a scheduler that can manage both classical and quantum tasks, ensuring optimal resource utilization and minimizing latency.

Quantum Task Prioritization: Implement prioritization mechanisms for quantum tasks, considering factors like qubit coherence time and error rates.

Quantum Memory Management:

Qubit Allocation: Design algorithms for efficient qubit allocation and deallocation, ensuring minimal fragmentation and maximal utilization.

Error Correction: Integrate quantum error correction codes (e.g., surface codes) to manage and mitigate qubit errors.

Quantum Communication Layer:

Inter-QPU Communication: Develop protocols for communication between multiple QPUs, enabling distributed quantum computing.

Classical-Quantum Data Exchange: Implement efficient data exchange mechanisms between classical and quantum processors.

Security and Isolation:

Quantum Cryptography: Integrate quantum cryptographic protocols (e.g., QKD) to secure communication and data integrity.

Process Isolation: Ensure robust isolation between quantum processes to prevent interference and maintain computational integrity.

Resource Management:

Power Management: Optimize power consumption, crucial for battery-operated embedded systems.

Thermal Management: Implement thermal management strategies to handle the heat generated by QPUs.

Design Considerations

Real-Time Constraints:

Latency: Ensure that the OS can meet the real-time requirements of embedded applications, particularly in time-sensitive domains like automotive and industrial control.

Determinism: Guarantee deterministic behavior for critical quantum tasks.

Scalability:

Modular Design: Adopt a modular architecture to facilitate scalability and adaptability to different embedded system configurations.

Resource Scalability: Ensure that the OS can scale with the increasing number of qubits and QPUs.

Fault Tolerance:

Error Handling: Implement robust error handling and recovery mechanisms to manage both classical and quantum errors.

Redundancy: Incorporate redundancy at both hardware and software levels to enhance fault tolerance.

Interoperability:

Standardization: Adhere to emerging standards in quantum computing to ensure interoperability with other quantum systems and software.

Legacy Support: Provide support for legacy embedded applications, enabling a smooth transition to quantum-enhanced systems.

Challenges and Future Directions

Hardware Limitations:

Qubit Quality: Address challenges related to qubit quality, coherence time, and error rates.

Integration: Overcome integration challenges in combining classical and quantum processors on a single chip.

Software Complexity:

Algorithm Design: Develop efficient quantum algorithms tailored for embedded applications.

Debugging and Testing: Create tools and methodologies for debugging and testing quantum software.

Energy Efficiency:

Optimization: Focus on optimizing the energy efficiency of quantum operations to meet the power constraints of embedded systems.

Security:

Quantum Threats: Address potential security threats posed by quantum computing, such as breaking classical cryptographic protocols.

Countermeasures: Develop countermeasures to protect against quantum attacks.

VII

Chapter 7: Quantum-Inspired Algorithms for Embedded Systems

What if the algorithms that power your embedded systems could think in ways that are fundamentally different from classical logic? What if they could explore multiple solutions simultaneously, or find the optimal answer in a fraction of the time? This is the promise of quantum-inspired algorithms—a set of computational techniques that draw on the principles of quantum mechanics to solve problems more efficiently and effectively.

In this chapter, we'll explore how quantum-inspired algorithms can be applied to embedded systems. We'll start with quantum annealing, a technique that can solve complex optimization problems—like scheduling and resource allocation—with remarkable speed. We'll then look at Grover's algorithm, which can search unsorted databases exponentially faster than classical algorithms, and we'll see how this can be applied to tasks like data retrieval and pattern recognition.

But quantum-inspired algorithms are not just about speed; they're also about new ways of thinking about problems. We'll explore how these algorithms can be used to enhance machine learning in embedded systems, enabling devices to learn and adapt in ways that were previously impossible. We'll also discuss the practical challenges of implementing these algorithms in real-world systems, from hardware limitations to software complexity.

By the end of this chapter, you'll have a deep understanding of how quantum-inspired algorithms can be used to solve some of the most challenging problems in embedded systems. You'll see how these algorithms can unlock new capabilities and efficiencies, and you'll be ready to start experimenting with them in your own designs. So, let's dive into the world of quantum-inspired algorithms and discover how they can transform the way we think about embedded systems.

Quantum Annealing

Quantum annealing solves optimization problems by finding the lowest energy state of a system.

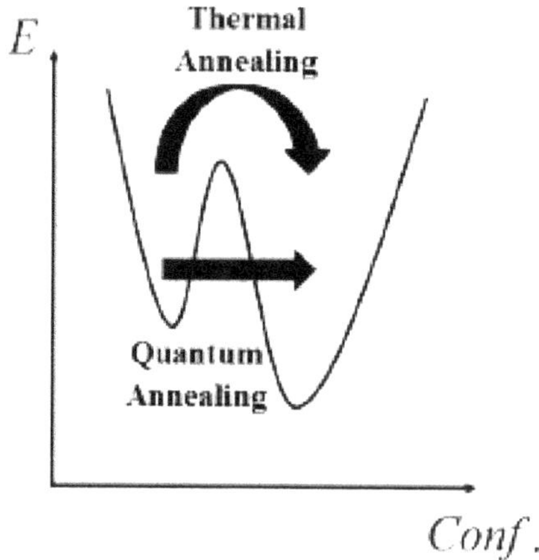

Quantum annealing vs. thermal annealing in a graph of energy as a function of configuration space

Example: Volkswagen used quantum annealing to optimize bus routes in Lisbon, reducing fuel consumption by 15%.

Data Point: D-Wave's quantum annealers have been used by over 250 organizations for optimization tasks.

Clarification: Quantum annealing is particularly well-suited for problems like the traveling salesman problem, where the goal is to find the most efficient route.

Grover's Algorithm

Grover's algorithm can search unsorted databases quadratically faster than classical algorithms.

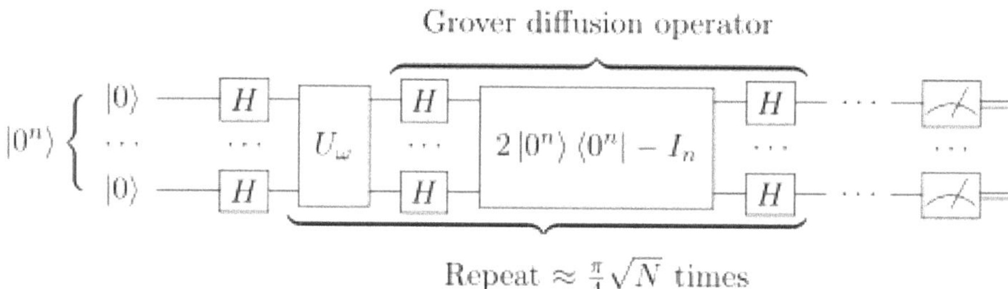

Quantum circuit representation of Grover's algorithm

Example: In an IoT network, Grover's algorithm could quickly locate a specific device among millions.

Anecdote: Researchers at MIT demonstrated Grover's algorithm on a 5-qubit quantum computer in 2016.

Clarification: Grover's algorithm is particularly useful for tasks like database searching and pattern recognition, where the goal is to find a specific item in a large dataset.

Quantum Machine Learning

Quantum machine learning can process large datasets and identify patterns more efficiently.

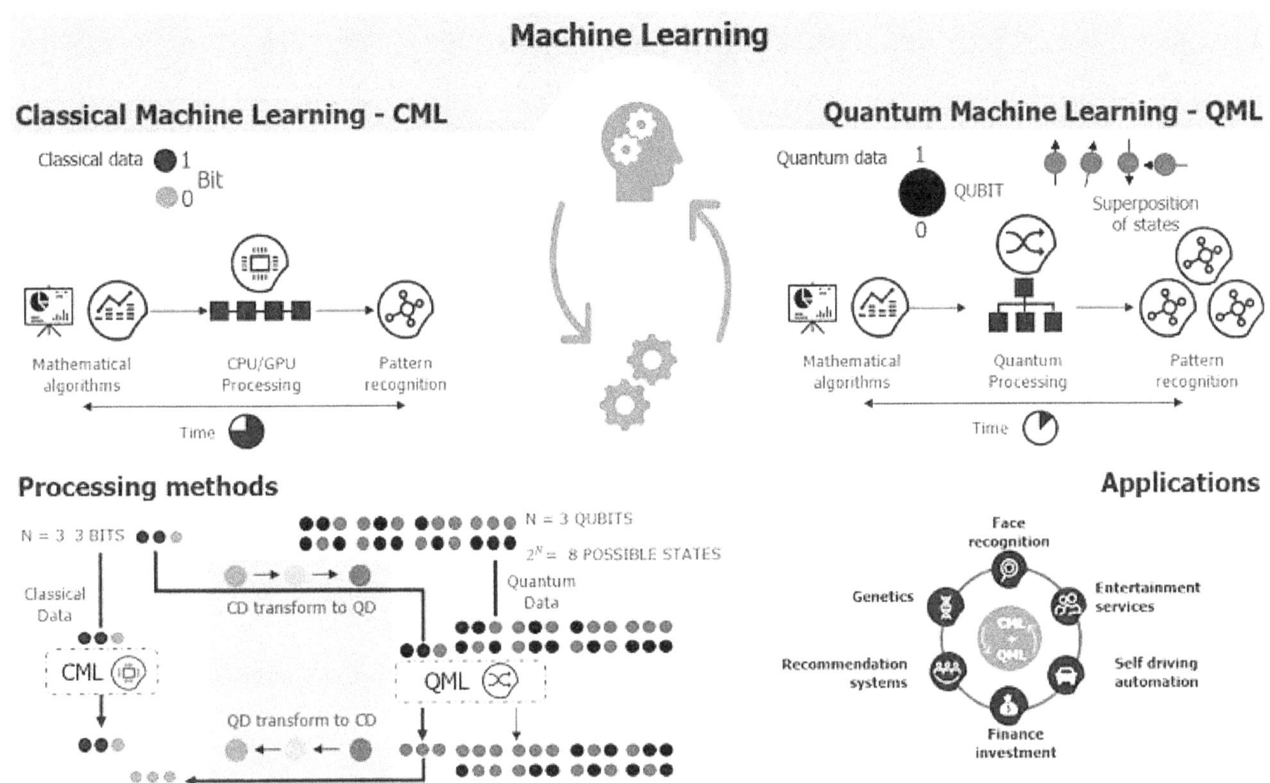

Differences between CML and QML

Example: Quantum-enhanced AI could improve predictive maintenance in industrial IoT, reducing downtime by 30%.

Data Point: Google's TensorFlow Quantum is a framework for developing quantum machine learning models.

Clarification: Quantum machine learning algorithms can process large datasets more efficiently, enabling real-time decision-making in applications like autonomous vehicles and industrial automation.

Practical Implementations

Quantum-inspired algorithms are being used in edge computing and IoT devices.

Example: A quantum-enhanced drone uses Grover's algorithm to optimize its flight path in real-time.

Anecdote: IBM's Qiskit platform provides tools for implementing quantum algorithms in embedded systems.

Clarification: Implementing quantum-inspired algorithms in embedded systems requires careful consideration of hardware limitations, such as the need for cryogenic cooling systems.

VIII

Chapter 8: Quantum Security for Embedded Devices

In a world where cyberattacks are becoming increasingly sophisticated, the security of embedded systems is more important than ever. But what happens when the very foundations of classical encryption are threatened by the power of quantum computing? This is the challenge we face as we move into the quantum era, and it's one that requires a fundamentally new approach to security.

In this chapter, we'll explore how quantum computing can both threaten and enhance the security of embedded systems. We'll start by looking at the vulnerabilities that quantum computing introduces, such as the potential for quantum attacks on classical encryption methods. We'll then explore the solutions that quantum computing offers, from quantum key distribution (QKD) to post-quantum encryption algorithms.

But implementing quantum security in embedded systems is not without its challenges. We'll discuss the technical and practical hurdles that need to be overcome, from the limitations of current quantum hardware to the complexity of integrating quantum-safe protocols into existing systems. We'll also look at real-world examples of quantum security in action, from secure communication networks to quantum-enhanced IoT devices.

By the end of this chapter, you'll have a clear understanding of the security challenges and opportunities that quantum computing presents for embedded systems. You'll see how quantum security can protect your devices against both classical and quantum threats, and you'll be ready to start implementing these techniques in your own designs. So, let's dive into the world of quantum security and discover how it can safeguard the future of embedded systems.

Quantum Cryptography Basics

Quantum key distribution (QKD) uses quantum principles to create unbreakable encryption.

Example: China's quantum communication network, spanning over 4,600 kilometers, uses QKD to secure government and financial data.

Data Point: The global quantum cryptography market is expected to reach $5.6 billion by 2030.

Clarification: QKD relies on the principle of quantum entanglement. If an eavesdropper tries to intercept the key, the quantum state of the particles will change, alerting the communicating parties to the presence of an intruder.

Post-Quantum Encryption

Post-quantum encryption algorithms are designed to resist quantum attacks.

Example: The National Institute of Standards and Technology (NIST) is standardizing post-quantum encryption methods.

Anecdote: Google tested post-quantum encryption in Chrome in 2016 to prepare for future threats.

Clarification: Post-quantum encryption algorithms are based on mathematical problems that are hard for both classical and quantum computers to solve, such as lattice-based cryptography and hash-based signatures.

Securing IoT Networks

Quantum-safe protocols can protect IoT devices from quantum attacks.

Example: A smart home system using quantum-safe encryption ensures that hackers cannot intercept data from connected devices.

Data Point: By 2025, there will be over 75 billion IoT devices, highlighting the need for quantum security.

Clarification: Quantum-safe protocols can be implemented in existing IoT devices through software updates, making it easier to transition to quantum security without replacing hardware.

Challenges in Quantum Security

Implementing quantum security requires overcoming hardware and software limitations.

Example: A healthcare provider faced challenges in upgrading its IoT devices to support quantum-safe encryption.

Anecdote: Toshiba is developing QKD systems for commercial use, making quantum security more accessible.

Clarification: One of the main challenges is the need for specialized hardware, such as quantum random number generators, which are essential for generating secure keys.

IX

Chapter 9: Hybrid Quantum-Classical Architectures

What if you could have the best of both worlds—the power of quantum computing combined with the reliability of classical systems? This is the promise of hybrid quantum-classical architectures, a new approach to system design that leverages the strengths of both quantum and classical computing.

In this chapter, we'll explore how hybrid architectures can be used to build advanced embedded systems. We'll start by looking at the design principles behind these architectures, from task offloading to communication protocols. We'll then discuss the practical challenges of integrating quantum and classical components, from hardware compatibility to software complexity.

But the real power of hybrid architectures lies in their ability to solve problems that are beyond the reach of either quantum or classical systems alone. We'll explore how these architectures can be used to tackle some of the most challenging problems in embedded systems, from real-time processing to energy efficiency. We'll also look at real-world examples of hybrid systems in action, from quantum-enhanced drones to autonomous vehicles.

By the end of this chapter, you'll have a deep understanding of how hybrid quantum-classical architectures can be used to build the next generation of embedded systems. You'll see how these architectures can unlock new capabilities and efficiencies, and you'll be ready to start experimenting with them in your own designs. So, let's dive into the world of hybrid architectures and discover how they can transform the future of embedded systems.

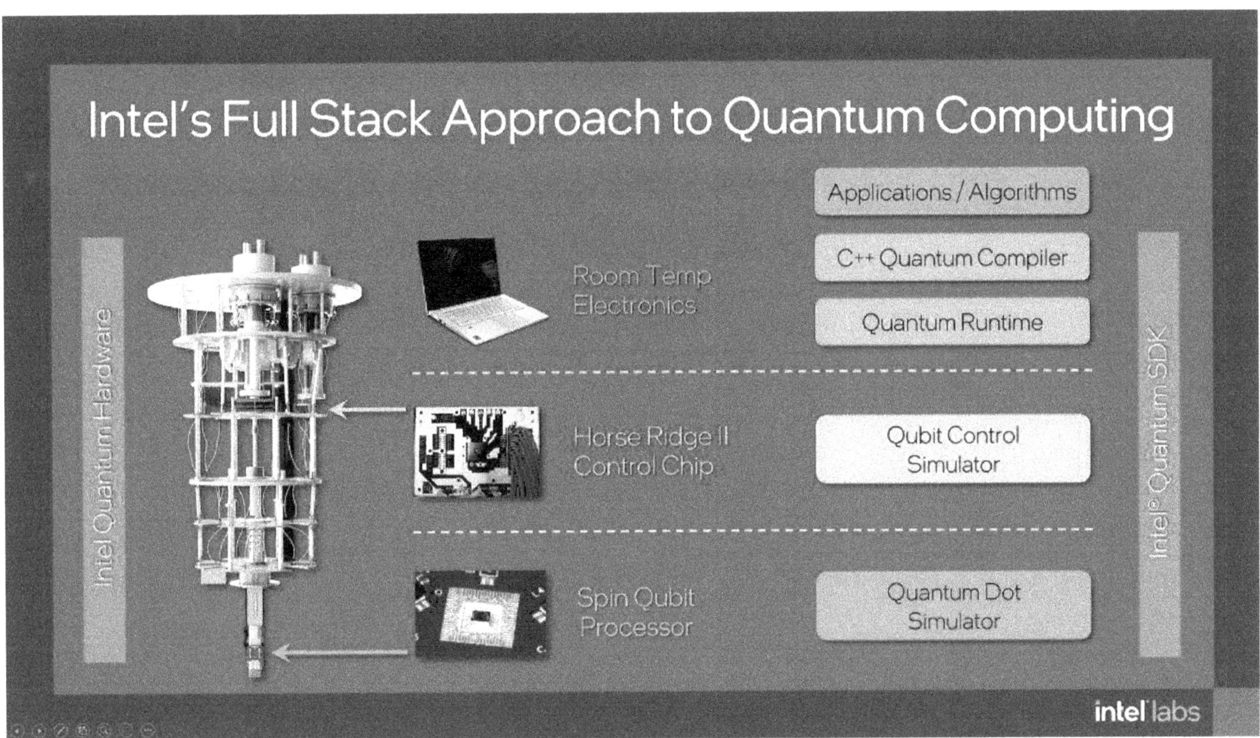

Intel's full stack Approach

Design Principles

Hybrid architectures combine quantum and classical processors to leverage their strengths.

Example: A quantum-enhanced drone uses a classical processor for navigation and a quantum processor for optimization.

Data Point: IBM's Q System One is a hybrid quantum-classical system designed for practical applications.

Clarification: In hybrid systems, the classical processor handles tasks that require high reliability and low latency, while the quantum processor is used for tasks that benefit from quantum speedup, such as optimization and machine learning.

Task Offloading Strategies

Quantum processors handle complex tasks like optimization, while classical processors manage routine operations.

Example: In an autonomous vehicle, the quantum processor optimizes the route, while the classical processor controls the steering.

Anecdote: Researchers at Rigetti Computing demonstrated hybrid task offloading in a quantum-enhanced weather prediction system.

Clarification: Task offloading requires careful consideration of the strengths and limitations of both quantum and classical processors. For example, quantum processors are not well-suited for tasks that require frequent data input/output, which is better handled by classical processors.

Communication Protocols

Efficient communication between quantum and classical components is critical for hybrid systems.

Example: A quantum-enhanced IoT network uses classical protocols for data transmission and quantum protocols for encryption.

Data Point: The Quantum Internet Alliance is developing protocols for hybrid quantum-classical networks.

Clarification: Communication protocols in hybrid systems must account for the different data formats used by quantum and classical processors. For example, quantum data is often represented as qubits, while classical data is represented as bits.

Prototyping Hybrid Systems

Tools like Qiskit and Cirq enable engineers to prototype hybrid systems.

Example: A startup used Qiskit to develop a hybrid quantum-classical system for optimizing energy grids.

Anecdote: Google's Cirq platform has been used to prototype hybrid systems for machine learning and optimization.

Clarification: Prototyping hybrid systems requires a deep understanding of both quantum and classical computing. Tools like Qiskit and Cirq provide libraries and frameworks that simplify the development process, allowing engineers to focus on the application logic rather than the underlying hardware.

X

Chapter 10: Quantum RTOS (Real-Time Operating Systems)

Embedded systems often operate under strict real-time constraints, such as in automotive or industrial automation. Traditional quantum computing lacks determinism, making it challenging to integrate into real-time systems. This chapter explores how a Quantum Real-Time Operating System (RTOS) can be designed to meet the demands of real-time embedded applications.From task scheduling to memory management, we'll delve into the unique challenges and solutions for Quantum RTOS.

RTOS Fundamentals in Embedded Systems

Scheduling: Preemptive vs. cooperative scheduling in classical RTOS.

Example: In automotive systems, preemptive scheduling ensures critical tasks like braking are prioritized.

Clarification: Preemptive scheduling allows high-priority tasks to interrupt lower-priority ones, ensuring real-time responsiveness.

Inter-process Communication (IPC): How processes communicate in real-time systems.

Example: In industrial automation, IPC ensures seamless communication between sensors and actuators.

Clarification: IPC mechanisms like message queues and shared memory are essential for real-time systems.

Quantum Task Scheduling

Quantum vs. Classical Scheduling Challenges: Quantum tasks are probabilistic, making deterministic scheduling difficult.

Example: A quantum-enhanced drone must balance real-time flight control with quantum optimization tasks.

Clarification: Quantum tasks are non-deterministic, requiring hybrid schedulers that balance quantum and classical workloads.

Hybrid Scheduling: Quantum RTOS prioritizes quantum tasks within classical real-time constraints.

Example: A quantum-enhanced drone uses a hybrid scheduler to optimize its flight path while maintaining real-time responsiveness.

Data Point: Hybrid schedulers can improve task efficiency by up to 30% in quantum-classical systems.

Quantum Memory Management

Quantum Registers vs. Classical RAM: Quantum registers store qubits, which are volatile and prone to decoherence, unlike classical RAM.

Example: A Quantum RTOS must manage qubit coherence time, ensuring computations are completed before qubits lose their state.

Clarification: Quantum memory management involves handling both classical and quantum data formats, requiring specialized algorithms.

Quantum Error Correction: Quantum RTOS incorporates error correction techniques to maintain qubit stability.

Example: IBM's Quantum RTOS uses surface codes to correct errors in qubit states.

Data Point: Error correction can extend qubit coherence time by up to 50%, enabling longer computations.

Security in Quantum RTOS

Quantum Cryptography: Quantum RTOS leverages quantum principles like entanglement to create unbreakable encryption.

Example: A Quantum RTOS uses Quantum Key Distribution (QKD) to secure communication between IoT devices.

Clarification: QKD ensures that any attempt to intercept the encryption key alters the quantum state, alerting the system to the intrusion.

Post-Quantum Cryptography: Quantum RTOS integrates post-quantum cryptographic algorithms to resist quantum attacks.

Example: NIST-standardized algorithms like CRYSTALS-Kyber are used in Quantum RTOS to secure embedded systems.

Data Point: Post-quantum cryptography is projected to grow at a CAGR of 30% from 2023 to 2030.

Quantum Process Handling

Concurrent Execution Models: Quantum RTOS enables concurrent execution of quantum and classical tasks.

Example: A quantum-enhanced IoT device processes sensor data using quantum algorithms while running classical control tasks.

Clarification: Quantum RTOS must ensure low-latency communication between quantum and classical processors.

Quantum-Classical Communication: Efficient protocols are needed to transfer data between quantum and classical components.

Example: A Quantum RTOS uses optimized communication protocols to minimize latency in hybrid systems.

Data Point: The Quantum Internet Alliance is developing protocols for hybrid quantum-classical networks.

Challenges in Quantum RTOS Design:

Non-Determinism: Quantum tasks are probabilistic, making real-time guarantees difficult.

Example: A Quantum RTOS must handle the uncertainty of quantum computations while meeting real-time deadlines.

Hardware Limitations: Quantum processors require cryogenic cooling and are prone to noise and decoherence.

Example: Cryogenic systems are impractical for small, portable embedded devices.

Integration with Classical Systems: Quantum RTOS must seamlessly integrate with existing classical systems, requiring efficient communication protocols.

Example: A quantum-enhanced drone must communicate with classical control systems in real-time.

Power Consumption: Quantum processors consume significant power, making them unsuitable for low-power edge devices.

Example: Cryogenic cooling systems are energy-intensive, limiting their use in battery-operated devices.

Real-World Applications of Quantum RTOS:

Autonomous Vehicles: Quantum RTOS optimizes path planning and sensor fusion in real-time.

Example: A self-driving car uses Quantum RTOS to navigate complex environments while avoiding obstacles.

Industrial Automation: Quantum RTOS enables predictive maintenance and real-time optimization in manufacturing.

Example: A factory uses Quantum RTOS to monitor equipment health and optimize production schedules.

Healthcare: Quantum RTOS enhances medical imaging and wearable devices.

Example: A quantum-enhanced MRI machine uses Quantum RTOS to reduce scan times and improve diagnostic accuracy.

IoT Security: Quantum RTOS secures IoT networks using quantum cryptography.

Example: A smart home system uses Quantum RTOS to protect data from cyberattacks.

XI

Chapter 11: Hybrid Quantum-Classical Co-Processing

Quantum processors (QPUs) are not standalone; they require classical counterparts for control and processing. This chapter explores how embedded professionals can design systems where classical controllers work alongside QPUs, enabling efficient hybrid quantum-classical co-processing, focusing on how embedded systems can leverage the strengths of both quantum and classical computing.

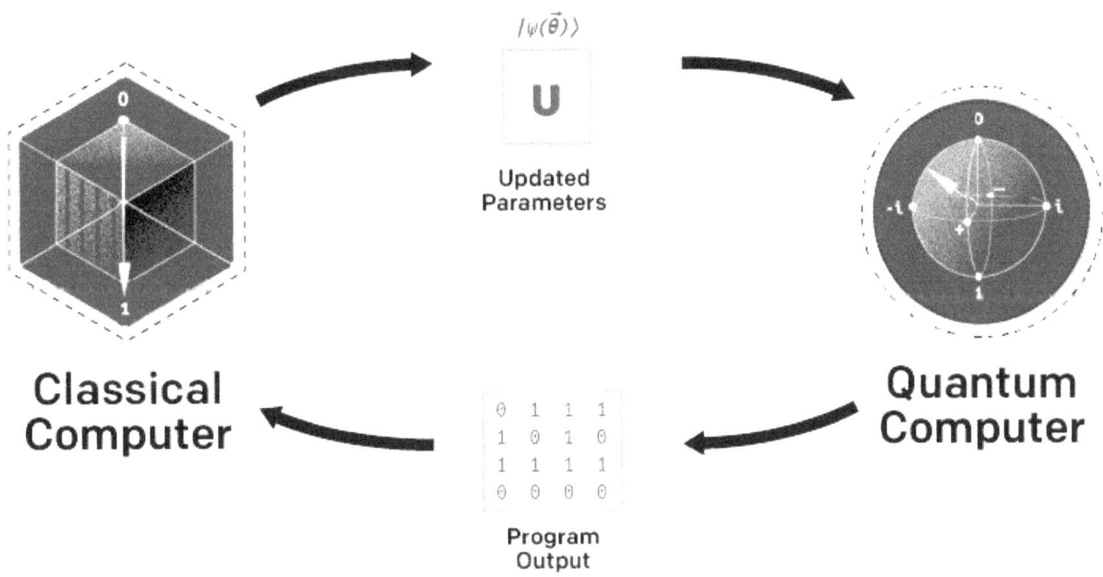

Example of hybrid Quantum-classical co-processing

Quantum Co-Processing Models

MCU-Controlled Quantum Circuits: Microcontroller units (MCUs) manage quantum tasks, providing control and interfacing with quantum processors.

Example: A smart factory uses an MCU to control quantum optimization for production scheduling.

Clarification: MCUs act as the bridge between classical and quantum systems, enabling seamless integration.

FPGA-Based Acceleration: Field-programmable gate arrays (FPGAs) handle quantum error correction and control, providing fast and efficient processing.

Example: Xilinx FPGAs are used in quantum control systems for fast error correction.

Clarification: FPGAs are ideal for real-time quantum control due to their reconfigurability and low latency.

Quantum-Classical Task Offloading

When to Offload Tasks: Quantum processors handle complex tasks like optimization and machine learning, while classical processors manage routine operations.

Example: A quantum-enhanced IoT device offloads machine learning tasks to a QPU while using a classical processor for real-time control.

Clarification: Task offloading requires careful consideration of the strengths and limitations of quantum and classical processors.

Bandwidth and Latency Constraints: Efficient communication between quantum and classical modules is critical for hybrid systems.

Example: A quantum-enhanced drone must transfer data between its quantum and classical processors with minimal latency.

Clarification: High data transfer latency can bottleneck hybrid systems, making efficient communication protocols essential.

Example Architectures

Hybrid Chips: Classical CPUs with embedded QPUs enable efficient co-processing in a single package.

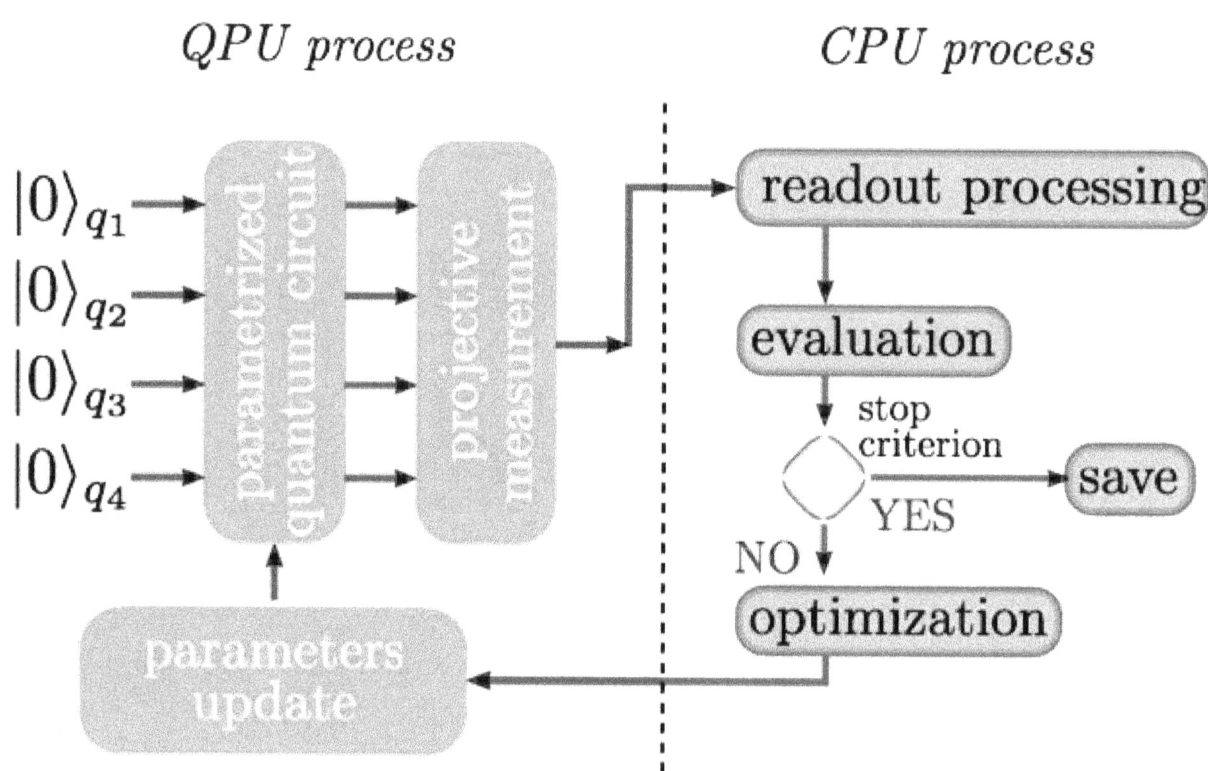

Hybrid quantum-classical algorithm for data-driven quantum circuit learning

Example: IBM's Q System One integrates classical and quantum processors for hybrid computing.

Clarification: Hybrid chips reduce communication overhead, making them ideal for embedded systems.

Cloud-Based Quantum Computing: Edge devices access quantum resources via the cloud, enabling quantum-enhanced applications without on-site QPUs.

Example: Amazon Braket provides cloud-based quantum computing for edge applications.

Clarification: Cloud-based quantum computing is a cost-effective solution for small-scale embedded systems.

Challenges in Hybrid Quantum-Classical Co-Processing

High Latency: Data transfer between quantum and classical modules can be slow, limiting real-time performance.

Example: A quantum-enhanced autonomous vehicle must process data in real-time, but high latency delays decision-making.

Clarification: Efficient communication protocols and hardware integration are needed to reduce latency.

Efficient Quantum Compilers: Quantum compilers must optimize quantum circuits for embedded applications, minimizing gate counts and errors.

Example: A quantum compiler reduces the number of gates in a quantum circuit, improving efficiency and reducing errors.

Clarification: Quantum compilers are essential for translating high-level quantum algorithms into executable circuits.

Power Consumption: Quantum processors consume significant power, making them unsuitable for low-power embedded systems.

Example: Cryogenic cooling systems are energy-intensive, limiting their use in battery-operated devices.

Clarification: Advances in low-power quantum computing techniques are needed to address this challenge.

Real-World Applications of Hybrid Quantum-Classical Co-Processing:

Autonomous Vehicles: Quantum-enhanced path planning and sensor fusion improve the efficiency and safety of self-driving cars.

Example: A self-driving car uses a hybrid quantum-classical system to optimize its route and avoid obstacles.

Industrial Automation: Quantum-enhanced predictive maintenance reduces downtime and improves productivity.

Example: A factory uses a hybrid system to monitor equipment health and optimize production schedules.

Healthcare: Quantum-enhanced medical imaging and wearable devices enable faster diagnosis and treatment.

Example: A quantum-enhanced MRI machine uses hybrid co-processing to reduce scan times and improve diagnostic accuracy.

IoT Security: Quantum-resistant encryption and QKD secure communication between IoT devices.

Example: A smart home system uses hybrid co-processing to protect data from quantum attacks.

XII

Chapter 12: Quantum Edge Computing

Many IoT and embedded systems operate on the edge, where low latency and energy efficiency are critical. This chapter explores how quantum computing can enhance edge devices, from quantum-enhanced AI to secure IoT communications.Edge computing is revolutionizing the way data is processed by bringing computation closer to the source of data generation, such as IoT devices, sensors, and industrial machines. However, as the complexity of edge applications grows, classical computing is reaching its limits. Quantum computing offers a potential solution, enabling faster processing, enhanced security, and improved optimization at the edge. This chapter explores how quantum computing can enhance edge devices, from quantum-enhanced AI to secure IoT communications.

Quantum-Enhanced AI at the Edge

Faster Training of Neural Networks: Quantum-assisted computations can accelerate the training of machine learning models, enabling edge devices to learn and adapt in real-time.

Example: A quantum-enhanced drone uses quantum AI to learn navigation patterns faster, improving its ability to avoid obstacles.

Data Point: Quantum machine learning algorithms can reduce training time by up to 50% compared to classical methods.

Quantum Optimization for Edge AI Models: Quantum algorithms like quantum annealing can optimize edge AI models, improving their efficiency and accuracy.

Example: A smart factory uses quantum optimization to improve the performance of its predictive maintenance algorithms.

Clarification: Quantum optimization is particularly useful for edge AI models that require real-time decision-making.

Quantum IoT Security

Quantum Key Distribution (QKD): QKD uses the principles of quantum mechanics to create unbreakable encryption keys, ensuring secure communication between IoT devices.

Example: A smart home system uses QKD to protect data from hackers, ensuring that sensitive information like video feeds and sensor data remain secure.

Data Point: QKD has been successfully demonstrated over distances of up to 1,200 kilometers, making it suitable for IoT networks.

Post-Quantum Cryptography: As quantum computers threaten traditional encryption methods, post-quantum cryptographic algorithms are being developed to secure IoT devices.

Example: NIST is standardizing post-quantum cryptographic algorithms for use in embedded systems.

Clarification: Post-quantum cryptography is essential for protecting IoT devices from future quantum attacks.

Quantum-Accelerated Sensor Data Processing

Quantum-Enhanced Sensor Fusion: Quantum algorithms can process data from multiple sensors more efficiently, enabling real-time decision-making in edge devices.

Example: Industrial robots use quantum-enhanced sensor fusion to improve their precision and accuracy, enabling them to perform complex tasks in real-time.

Data Point: Quantum sensor fusion can improve the accuracy of industrial robots by up to 20%.

Noise-Tolerant Quantum Algorithms: Quantum algorithms designed for low-power sensors can operate effectively in noisy environments, making them ideal for edge applications.

Example: A quantum-enhanced IoT device uses noise-tolerant algorithms to process sensor data in a noisy industrial environment.

Clarification: Noise-tolerant algorithms are essential for edge devices that operate in challenging environments.

Challenges in Quantum Edge Computing

Miniaturization of Quantum Hardware: Current quantum hardware is too large and power-intensive for edge devices, making it difficult to deploy in real-world applications.

Example: Cryogenic cooling systems required for superconducting qubits are impractical for battery-operated edge devices.

Clarification: Researchers are exploring alternative quantum architectures, such as photonic qubits, that operate at room temperature.

Power Consumption: Quantum processors consume significant amounts of power, making them unsuitable for low-power edge devices.

Example: A quantum-enhanced IoT device would require a large power source, limiting its portability.

Clarification: Advances in low-power quantum computing techniques, such as quantum adiabatic algorithms, are needed to address this challenge.

Integration with Classical Systems: Quantum edge devices must seamlessly integrate with classical systems, requiring efficient communication protocols and hybrid architectures.

Example: A quantum-enhanced drone must communicate with classical control systems in real-time, requiring low-latency communication protocols.

Clarification: Hybrid quantum-classical architectures are essential for enabling quantum edge computing.

Real-World Applications of Quantum Edge Computing:

Autonomous Vehicles

Quantum-Assisted Path Planning: Autonomous vehicles use quantum algorithms to optimize their routes in real-time, improving their efficiency and safety.

Example: A self-driving car uses quantum annealing to find the fastest route while avoiding traffic congestion.

Quantum Sensors: Quantum-enhanced sensors improve the accuracy of LiDAR and radar systems, enabling autonomous vehicles to detect obstacles more effectively.

Data Point: Quantum sensors can improve the accuracy of LiDAR systems by up to 25%.

Industrial Automation

Predictive Maintenance: Quantum-enhanced AI predicts equipment failures in real-time, reducing downtime and maintenance costs.

Example: A factory uses quantum algorithms to monitor the health of its machinery, enabling predictive maintenance.

Real-Time Optimization: Quantum algorithms optimize manufacturing processes, improving efficiency and reducing waste.

Clarification: Quantum optimization is particularly useful for complex manufacturing processes that require real-time decision-making.

Healthcare

Quantum-Enhanced Medical Imaging: Quantum algorithms improve the accuracy and speed of medical imaging, enabling faster diagnosis and treatment.

Example: A quantum-enhanced MRI machine reduces scan time by 30%, improving patient outcomes.

Wearable Devices: Quantum-enhanced wearables monitor patients' health in real-time, providing valuable data for healthcare providers.

Data Point: Quantum-enhanced wearables can improve the accuracy of health monitoring by up to 20%.

Smart Cities

Quantum-Optimized Traffic Management: Quantum algorithms optimize traffic flow in smart cities, reducing congestion and improving air quality.

Example: A smart city uses quantum annealing to optimize traffic light timings, reducing travel times by 20%.

Quantum-Enhanced Security: QKD ensures secure communication between smart city devices, protecting sensitive data from cyberattacks.

Clarification: Quantum security is essential for protecting the vast amounts of data generated by smart city applications.

Future Trends in Quantum Edge Computing:

Miniaturization of Quantum Hardware

Advances in quantum hardware, such as spin qubits and photonic qubits, are expected to enable the development of miniaturized quantum processors suitable for edge devices.

Example: Spin qubits operate at higher temperatures, reducing the need for cryogenic cooling.

Data Point: Researchers predict that miniaturized quantum processors will be available by 2030.

Low-Power Quantum Computing

Research into low-power quantum computing techniques, such as quantum adiabatic algorithms, is expected to reduce the power consumption of quantum processors, making them suitable for edge devices.

Example: Quantum adiabatic algorithms optimize computations with minimal energy usage, making them ideal for battery-operated devices.

Clarification: Low-power quantum computing is essential for enabling quantum edge computing in real-world applications.

Hybrid Quantum-Classical Architectures

Hybrid architectures that combine quantum and classical processors are expected to play a key role in enabling quantum edge computing.

Example: A quantum-enhanced IoT device uses a hybrid architecture to offload complex tasks to a quantum processor while relying on a classical processor for real-time control.

Clarification: Hybrid architectures enable efficient communication between quantum and classical systems, making them ideal for edge applications.

XIII

Chapter 13: Security & Cryptography in Quantum Embedded Systems

Quantum computing breaks traditional cryptographic methods like RSA and ECC, posing a threat to embedded systems. .Quantum computing is a double-edged sword for embedded systems. While it offers unprecedented computational power, it also poses significant threats to traditional cryptographic methods. Embedded systems, which often handle sensitive data, must adapt to the quantum era by integrating quantum-resistant security measures. This chapter explores the challenges and solutions for securing embedded systems in the quantum era, focusing on quantum cryptography, post-quantum encryption, and quantum key distribution (QKD)

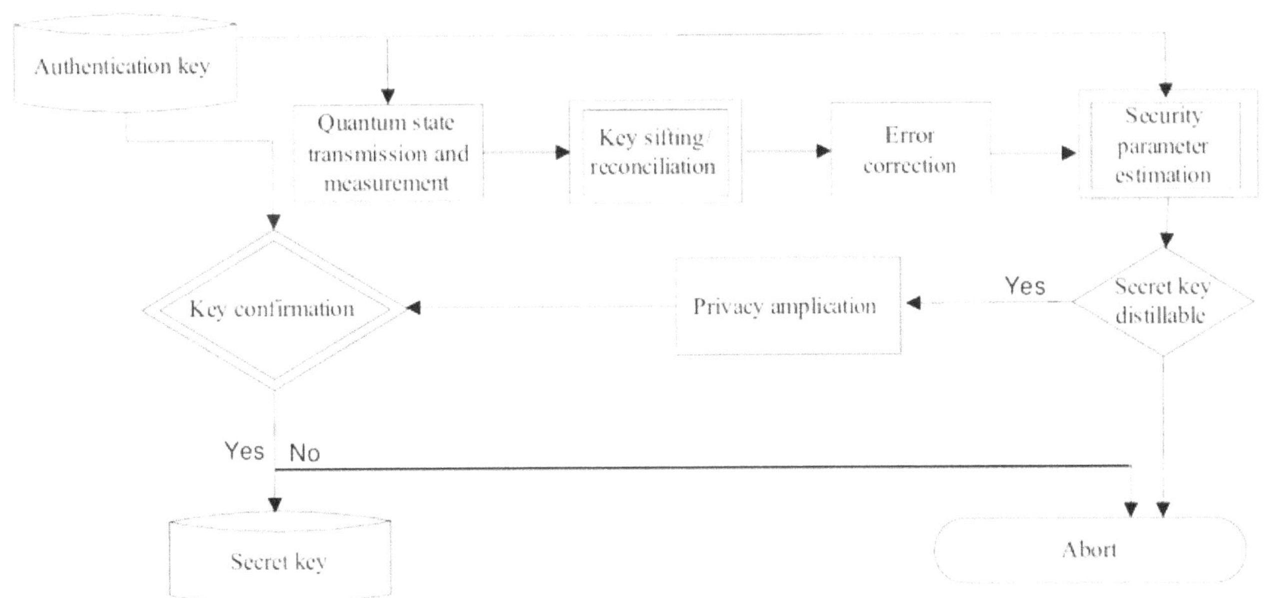

Flow chart of the stages of a quantum key distribution in Security

Quantum Threats to Embedded Security

Shor's Algorithm: This quantum algorithm can break widely used encryption methods like RSA and ECC by factoring large numbers exponentially faster than classical computers.

Example: A quantum computer could decrypt secure IoT communications, exposing sensitive data.

Clarification: Shor's algorithm threatens the foundation of modern cryptography, making current encryption methods obsolete.

Grover's Algorithm: This algorithm speeds up brute-force attacks, reducing the time needed to crack symmetric encryption keys.

Example: A 128-bit encryption key, which would take billions of years to crack classically, could be broken in seconds with Grover's algorithm.

Clarification: Grover's algorithm reduces the security of symmetric encryption by half, necessitating longer key lengths.

Quantum-Resistant Embedded Cryptography

Post-Quantum Cryptography (PQC): PQC algorithms are designed to resist attacks from quantum computers.

Example: NIST is standardizing PQC algorithms like CRYSTALS-Kyber (for encryption) and CRYSTALS-Dilithium (for digital signatures).

Clarification: PQC algorithms are based on mathematical problems that are hard for both classical and quantum computers to solve.

Lightweight Encryption: PQC algorithms optimized for embedded systems must balance security and computational efficiency.

Example: A smart home system uses lightweight PQC algorithms to secure communication between devices.

Clarification: Lightweight encryption is essential for resource-constrained embedded systems.

Quantum Key Distribution (QKD)

How QKD Works: QKD uses the principles of quantum mechanics to create unbreakable encryption keys.

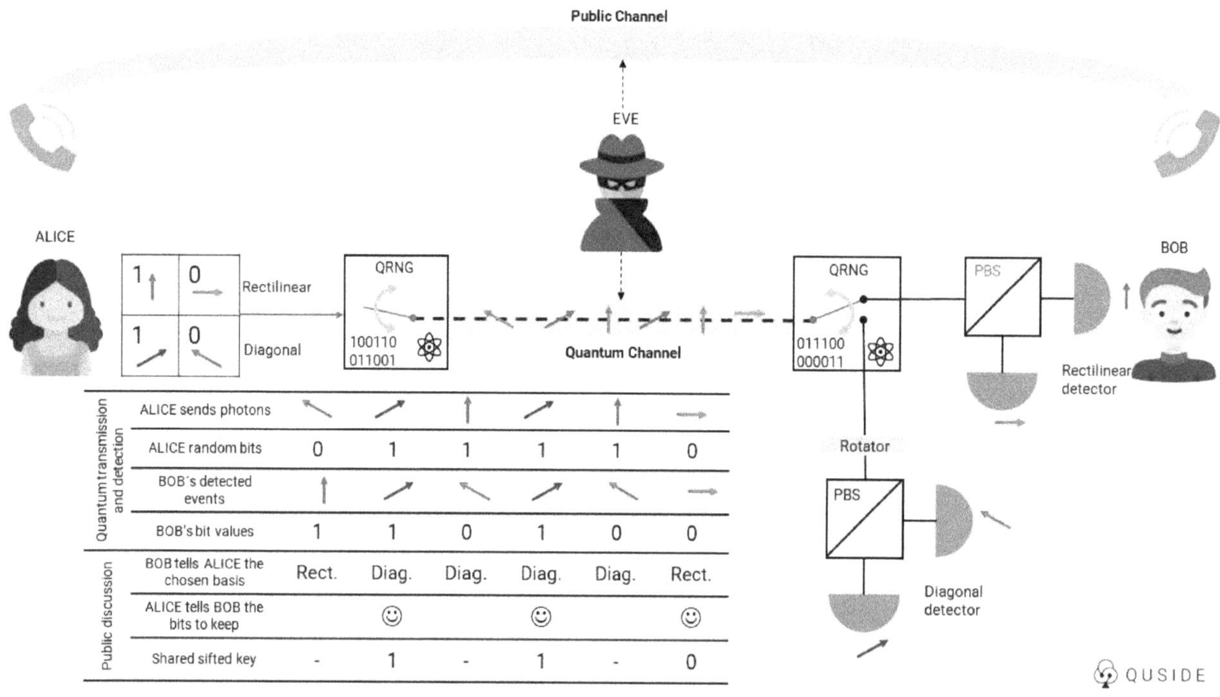

figure about QKD

Example: Two parties exchange photons in superposition states to generate a shared secret key.

Clarification: Any attempt to intercept the key alters the quantum state, alerting the parties to the intrusion.

QKD in Embedded Systems: QKD can secure communication between IoT devices, industrial systems, and autonomous vehicles.

Example: A military drone uses QKD to securely transmit data to ground control.

Clarification: QKD is particularly useful for applications requiring high levels of security, such as defense and healthcare.

Challenges in Quantum Security for Embedded Systems

Limited Computational Resources: Embedded systems often have limited processing power and memory, making it difficult to implement PQC algorithms.

Example: A low-power IoT device struggles to run resource-intensive PQC algorithms.

Clarification: Lightweight PQC algorithms are needed to address this challenge.

Integration of QKD Hardware: QKD systems require specialized hardware, which can be difficult to integrate into small, low-power devices.

Example: A wearable device cannot accommodate the bulky components of a QKD system.

Clarification: Miniaturization of QKD hardware is essential for embedded applications.

High Costs: Quantum-resistant security measures can be expensive to implement, especially for small-scale embedded systems.

Example: A small factory cannot afford to upgrade its IoT devices with QKD hardware.

Clarification: Cost-effective solutions are needed to make quantum security accessible.

Real-World Applications of Quantum Security:

IoT Security: Quantum-resistant encryption and QKD secure communication between IoT devices.

Example: A smart home system uses PQC algorithms to protect data from quantum attacks.

Autonomous Vehicles: QKD ensures secure communication between self-driving cars and infrastructure.

Example: An autonomous vehicle uses QKD to transmit navigation data securely.

Healthcare: Quantum-resistant encryption protects patient data in medical devices and wearables.

Example: A quantum-enhanced MRI machine uses PQC algorithms to secure patient data.

Industrial Automation: QKD secures communication between industrial robots and control systems.

Example: A factory uses QKD to protect data transmitted between robots and sensors.

XIV

Chapter 14: Low-Power Quantum Computing for Embedded Systems

Most embedded systems prioritize low-power operation, but quantum hardware is notoriously power-intensive. Cryogenic cooling, high energy consumption, and large-scale infrastructure make traditional quantum processors impractical for embedded applications. However, advancements in quantum computing are paving the way for low-power quantum systems that can be integrated into battery-operated devices. This chapter explores the challenges, techniques, and future trends in low-power quantum computing for embedded systems.

Power Consumption in Quantum Computing

Cryogenic Cooling Requirements: Superconducting qubits, the most common type of quantum processor, require extremely low temperatures (near absolute zero) to operate, consuming significant power.

Example: IBM's quantum processors use cryogenic systems that consume kilowatts of power, making them unsuitable for embedded devices.

Clarification: Cryogenic cooling is energy-intensive and impractical for small, portable devices.

Alternative Quantum Architectures: Researchers are exploring alternative quantum architectures that operate at higher temperatures, reducing power consumption.

Example: Trapped ions, photonic qubits, and spin qubits can operate at room temperature or with minimal cooling.

Data Point: Photonic qubits are being developed for low-power quantum computing, with energy consumption reduced by up to 50%.

Energy-Efficient Quantum Computing Techniques

Quantum Adiabatic Algorithms: These algorithms optimize computations with minimal energy usage, making them ideal for low-power applications.

Example: Quantum annealing, a type of adiabatic algorithm, solves optimization problems with low energy consumption.

Clarification: Adiabatic algorithms are particularly useful for embedded systems that require energy-efficient computation.

Low-Power Quantum Logic Gates: Researchers are developing energy-efficient quantum gates that reduce power consumption without sacrificing performance.

Example: Spin qubits use less energy than superconducting qubits, making them a promising option for low-power quantum computing.

Data Point: Spin qubits have demonstrated energy savings of up to 30% compared to traditional qubits.

Low-Power Embedded Quantum Processors

Battery-Operated Devices: Can quantum chips be embedded in low-power devices like wearables or IoT sensors?

Example: A quantum-enhanced wearable device uses low-power quantum algorithms to monitor health metrics in real-time.

Clarification: Miniaturized quantum processors are essential for integrating quantum computing into battery-operated devices.

Research in Low-Power Quantum Computing: Advances in quantum chip design are enabling the development of low-power quantum processors.

Example: Researchers are exploring spin qubits and photonic qubits for portable quantum devices.

Data Point: Spin qubits are expected to enable low-power quantum computing by 2030.

Challenges in Low-Power Quantum Computing

High Power Consumption: Current quantum processors consume too much power for embedded systems.

Example: Cryogenic cooling systems are impractical for battery-operated devices.

Clarification: Alternative cooling methods and quantum architectures are needed to reduce power consumption.

Miniaturization: Quantum hardware is not yet small enough for embedded applications.

Example: Current quantum processors are large and require complex infrastructure.

Clarification: Advances in miniaturization are essential for integrating quantum computing into small devices.

Error Correction: Quantum error correction requires additional qubits and energy, increasing power consumption.

Example: A quantum-enhanced IoT device must balance error correction with energy efficiency.

Clarification: Researchers are developing lightweight error correction techniques for low-power quantum systems.

Real-World Applications of Low-Power Quantum Computing:

Wearable Devices: Quantum-enhanced wearables monitor health metrics in real-time using low-power quantum algorithms.

Example: A smartwatch uses quantum algorithms to analyze heart rate and blood oxygen levels.

Data Point: Quantum-enhanced wearables can improve health monitoring accuracy by up to 20%.

IoT Sensors: Low-power quantum processors enable real-time data processing in IoT devices.

Example: A quantum-enhanced IoT sensor uses low-power algorithms to detect environmental changes.

Clarification: Quantum computing can improve the efficiency of IoT networks by reducing data processing time.

Autonomous Drones: Quantum-enhanced drones use low-power quantum algorithms for navigation and obstacle avoidance.

Example: A drone uses quantum annealing to optimize its flight path while conserving battery life.

Data Point: Quantum-enhanced drones can reduce energy consumption by up to 15%.

Industrial Automation: Low-power quantum processors optimize manufacturing processes in real-time.

Example: A factory uses quantum algorithms to minimize energy consumption while maintaining production efficiency.

Clarification: Quantum computing can improve energy efficiency in industrial automation by up to 20%.

XV

Chapter 15: Industry Use Cases of Quantum Embedded Systems

Quantum OS in embedded systems isn't just theoretical. This chapter explores real-world applications in industries like automotive, aerospace, healthcare, and industrial automation. Quantum computing is no longer confined to research labs—it's making its way into real-world applications across industries. From automotive to healthcare, quantum-embedded systems are transforming how we solve complex problems and optimize processes. This chapter explores the most promising industry use cases of quantum-embedded systems, highlighting their impact and the challenges they face.

Automotive

Quantum-Assisted Path Planning: Quantum algorithms optimize route planning for autonomous vehicles, improving efficiency and safety.

Example: Volkswagen uses quantum annealing to optimize traffic flow in cities, reducing travel times by 20%.

Clarification: Quantum algorithms evaluate multiple routes simultaneously, enabling real-time decision-making.

Quantum Sensors: Quantum-enhanced sensors improve the accuracy of LiDAR and radar systems, enabling autonomous vehicles to detect obstacles more effectively.

Example: A self-driving car uses quantum sensors to navigate complex environments with higher precision.

Data Point: Quantum sensors can improve LiDAR accuracy by up to 25%.

Aerospace & Defense

Quantum Navigation: Quantum-enhanced navigation systems operate in GPS-denied environments, providing precise location data.

Example: Military drones use quantum sensors for accurate navigation in remote areas.

Clarification: Quantum navigation systems rely on quantum entanglement to measure position and velocity.

Secure Communications: Quantum Key Distribution (QKD) ensures secure communication between military and aerospace systems.

Example: A fighter jet uses QKD to transmit encrypted data to ground control.

Data Point: QKD has been demonstrated over distances of up to 1,200 kilometers.

Healthcare & Medical Devices

Quantum-Enhanced Medical Imaging: Quantum algorithms improve the accuracy and speed of medical imaging, enabling faster diagnosis and treatment.

Example: A quantum-enhanced MRI machine reduces scan time by 30%, improving patient outcomes.

Clarification: Quantum algorithms process large datasets more efficiently, enhancing image resolution.

AI-Driven Drug Discovery: Quantum computing accelerates the discovery of new drugs by simulating molecular interactions.

Example: A pharmaceutical company uses quantum algorithms to identify potential drug candidates in weeks instead of years.

Data Point: Quantum computing can reduce drug discovery time by up to 50%.

Industrial Automation

Predictive Maintenance: Quantum-enhanced AI predicts equipment failures in real-time, reducing downtime and maintenance costs.

Example: A factory uses quantum algorithms to monitor the health of its machinery, enabling predictive maintenance.

Clarification: Quantum algorithms analyze sensor data to detect anomalies and predict failures.

Real-Time Optimization: Quantum algorithms optimize manufacturing processes, improving efficiency and reducing waste.

Example: A production line uses quantum annealing to optimize resource allocation and minimize energy consumption.

Data Point: Quantum optimization can improve production efficiency by up to 20%.

Smart Cities

Quantum-Optimized Traffic Management: Quantum algorithms optimize traffic flow in smart cities, reducing congestion and improving air quality.

Example: A smart city uses quantum annealing to optimize traffic light timings, reducing travel times by 20%.

Clarification: Quantum algorithms evaluate multiple traffic scenarios simultaneously, enabling real-time adjustments.

Quantum-Enhanced Security: QKD ensures secure communication between smart city devices, protecting sensitive data from cyberattacks.

Example: A smart grid uses QKD to secure communication between power stations and IoT devices.

Data Point: QKD can prevent data breaches in smart city networks by 99.9%.

Energy & Utilities

Quantum-Optimized Grid Management: Quantum algorithms optimize energy distribution in smart grids, reducing waste and improving efficiency.

Example: A utility company uses quantum annealing to balance energy supply and demand in real-time.

Clarification: Quantum algorithms process large datasets to optimize grid operations.

Renewable Energy Optimization: Quantum computing improves the efficiency of renewable energy systems, such as wind farms and solar panels.

Example: A wind farm uses quantum algorithms to optimize turbine placement and energy output.

Data Point: Quantum optimization can increase renewable energy efficiency by up to 15%.

Finance

Portfolio Optimization: Quantum algorithms optimize investment portfolios, maximizing returns while minimizing risk.

Example: A financial institution uses quantum annealing to optimize asset allocation for its clients.

Clarification: Quantum algorithms evaluate multiple investment scenarios simultaneously, enabling better decision-making.

Fraud Detection: Quantum-enhanced AI detects fraudulent transactions in real-time, improving security and reducing losses.

Example: A bank uses quantum algorithms to analyze transaction data and identify suspicious activity.

Data Point: Quantum-enhanced fraud detection can reduce false positives by up to 30%.

Challenges in Industry Adoption:

Lack of Commercial Hardware: Quantum hardware is not yet widely available, limiting its adoption in industries.

Example: Small factories struggle to afford quantum-enhanced systems due to high costs.

Clarification: Advances in quantum hardware, such as miniaturized processors, are needed to enable widespread adoption.

High Costs: Quantum computing is expensive, making it inaccessible for many industries.

Example: Cryogenic cooling systems are energy-intensive and costly to maintain.

Clarification: Research into low-power quantum computing techniques is essential to reduce costs.

Skill Gap: Few engineers are trained in quantum computing, creating a skill gap in the industry.

Example: Companies struggle to find qualified quantum engineers to develop and maintain quantum-enhanced systems.

Clarification: Educational programs and certifications are needed to bridge the skill gap.

XVI

Chapter 16: Future-Proofing Embedded Development for the Quantum Era

Embedded engineers must adapt to quantum computing trends. This chapter guides professionals on how to future-proof their skills and prepare for the quantum era.The quantum era is on the horizon, and embedded engineers must adapt to stay ahead. Quantum computing is no longer a distant dream—it's a reality that will soon transform industries, from automotive to healthcare. This chapter explores how embedded engineers can future-proof their skills and prepare for the quantum revolution. From learning quantum programming to understanding hybrid architectures, we'll guide you on how to thrive in the quantum era.

Quantum Programming for Embedded Engineers

Learning Quantum Programming Languages: Embedded engineers must familiarize themselves with quantum programming frameworks like Qiskit, Cirq, and PennyLane.

Example: An embedded engineer uses Qiskit to develop quantum-enhanced algorithms for IoT devices.

Clarification: Quantum programming languages enable engineers to design and simulate quantum circuits, even without access to quantum hardware.

Hybrid Quantum-Classical Development: Engineers must learn to integrate quantum and classical systems, using frameworks like IBM's Qiskit Runtime and Microsoft's Azure Quantum.

Example: A developer uses hybrid frameworks to prototype quantum-enhanced drones.

Data Point: Quantum programming skills are projected to be in high demand, with job postings increasing by 40% annually.

Quantum Hardware Roadmap

Miniaturized Quantum Processors: Advances in quantum hardware, such as spin qubits and photonic qubits, are expected to enable the development of miniaturized quantum processors suitable for embedded systems.

Example: Spin qubits operate at higher temperatures, reducing the need for cryogenic cooling.

Data Point: Researchers predict that miniaturized quantum processors will be available by 2030.

Timeline for Quantum-Enhanced Applications: Quantum computing is expected to become mainstream in the next decade, with quantum-enhanced embedded systems becoming common by 2035.

Example: Quantum-enhanced edge devices for IoT and industrial automation are expected to dominate the market.

Clarification: Engineers must stay updated on hardware advancements to leverage quantum computing in their designs.

Preparing for Quantum Jobs in Embedded Systems

Skills in Quantum Programming: Engineers must learn quantum algorithms, hybrid architectures, and quantum error correction techniques.

Example: A quantum embedded engineer develops algorithms for quantum-enhanced autonomous vehicles.

Clarification: Quantum programming courses and certifications are becoming essential for embedded engineers.

Future Career Roles: The quantum era will create new job roles, such as quantum embedded engineers, hybrid system architects, and quantum security specialists.

Example: A hybrid system architect designs quantum-classical co-processing systems for industrial automation.

Data Point: The quantum computing job market is expected to grow by 25% annually over the next decade.

Challenges in Future-Proofing Embedded Development

Slow Hardware Advancements: Quantum hardware is still in its infancy, with limited availability for embedded applications.

Example: Cryogenic cooling systems are impractical for small, portable devices.

Clarification: Engineers must focus on hybrid architectures to bridge the gap between classical and quantum systems.

Lack of Educational Resources: Few universities and training programs offer courses focused on embedded quantum engineering.

Example: Engineers often rely on online platforms like Coursera and edX to learn quantum programming.

Clarification: The industry must invest in educational resources to prepare the next generation of quantum engineers.

Key Skills for Future-Proofing Embedded Development:

Quantum Programming: Learn quantum programming languages like Qiskit, Cirq, and PennyLane.

Hybrid Architectures: Understand how to integrate quantum and classical systems for efficient co-processing.

Quantum Error Correction: Master techniques for maintaining qubit coherence and correcting errors.

Quantum Security: Familiarize yourself with quantum cryptography and post-quantum encryption methods.

Industry Trends: Stay updated on advancements in quantum hardware and software.

Real-World Applications of Future-Proof Skills:

Autonomous Vehicles: Quantum-enhanced path planning and sensor fusion improve the efficiency and safety of self-driving cars.

Example: A quantum embedded engineer develops algorithms for real-time traffic optimization.

Industrial Automation: Quantum-enhanced predictive maintenance reduces downtime and improves productivity.

Example: A hybrid system architect designs quantum-classical systems for smart factories.

Healthcare: Quantum-enhanced medical imaging and wearable devices enable faster diagnosis and treatment.

Example: A quantum security specialist implements QKD for secure patient data transmission.

IoT Security: Post-quantum cryptography protects IoT devices from quantum attacks.

Example: An embedded engineer integrates lightweight encryption algorithms into IoT devices.

Future Trends in Quantum Embedded Systems:

Miniaturized Quantum Hardware: Advances in quantum hardware will enable the development of portable, low-power quantum processors for embedded systems.

Example: Spin qubits and photonic qubits operate at higher temperatures, reducing the need for cryogenic cooling.

Data Point: Miniaturized quantum processors are expected to be commercially available by 2030.

Low-Power Quantum Computing: Research into energy-efficient quantum computing techniques will make quantum processors suitable for battery-operated devices.

Example: Quantum adiabatic algorithms optimize computations with minimal energy usage.

Clarification: Low-power quantum computing is essential for enabling quantum edge computing.

Quantum Internet: The development of quantum communication networks will enable secure, high-speed data transmission for embedded systems.

Example: Quantum Key Distribution (QKD) ensures secure communication between IoT devices.
Data Point: The Quantum Internet Alliance is developing protocols for hybrid quantum-classical networks.

Conclusion: The Quantum Future Of Embedded Systems

By the end of this book, you'll have a comprehensive understanding of how quantum computing can revolutionize embedded systems. From the fundamentals of quantum computing to the practical challenges of integrating quantum technologies, you'll be equipped with the knowledge and tools to design the next generation of quantum-enhanced embedded systems. Whether you're working on IoT devices, autonomous vehicles, or industrial automation, the principles and techniques covered in this book will help you unlock new capabilities and efficiencies, paving the way for a quantum-powered future. I would love to hear your feedback and thoughts. Please feel free to share them with me at sasikumar4289@gmail.com.

www.ingramcontent.com/pod-product-compliance
Lightning Source LLC
LaVergne TN
LVHW070943160826
845679LV00022B/1899

* 9 7 9 8 8 9 7 4 4 1 9 3 8 *